Beginners Paleo Diet Guide

How To Properly Implement The Paleo Diet

Delbert F. Dooley

Contents

Contents

Chapter One

Introduction

Many have thrown shade and ridiculed the paleo diet for a whole lot of reasons. One is that it is a cave man diet. Okay, so what if it is? We still do stuff that hails from the past. For instance, cavemen used to communicate through writing on the walls, similar to the current Facebook walls we use. Ooh well, not so similar but at least the concept is the same, or don't you think so too?

We cannot assume that the cavem an's favorite dish was tea bone steak, but also, we can't overrule that his favorite pass time had to be clubbing. Maybe he would even order a club sandwich occasionally, who knows. All the same, we sure owe a lot to our ancestors when it comes to the paleo diet.

This is a diet that, simply put, emulates the paleolithic era. This is a time when the agricultural revolution gathered ground to kickstart. Its principles rely on wholeSome eating of foods such as lean meat, fruits, vegetables, fish, seeds and nuts. You see, it's actually not a bad diet per se. So, rather than hitting the local stores, you can simply go hunting and gathering to save some bucks. Perhaps you could even get stoned and that's it, since it is a stone Age diet – just kidding.

The aim of such a diet is to trace our roots and try to emulate what was eaten in the past. PerSonal aims for this diet may include planning meals and weight loss. As far as diets are concerned, paleo is well-known and ranks up there with the likes of keto. You can argue that paleo it the most time-tested diet in history, as it goes back in time when cavemen still existed. In a nutshell, the diet means converting your house into a cave, not literally, but ideally. So, if a caveman didn't eat it, avoid it like the plague. It's probably not good for your health.

The foundation for the success of the paleo diet has to be the fact that cavemen survived for long without lifestyle diseases and proper meds. Pundits argue that there is limited research to support this and those genetics keep on changing. As much as it is a couple of years back, the genetics haven't changed that much. So, when did the rain start beating us? Well, after Netflix and chill. In other words, our lifestyle has made it difficult to live a perfectly normal and healthy mode.

The numbers of those weighing above the standard weight and getting to obese levels are constantly rising like the global warming scourge. And this is not a good sign for all of us. We can all agree to this point that we need a shift in our diet, to prevent diseases and boost weight control. So, is the paleo diet sustainable to help us achieve these goals? Let's find out in the subsequent chapter.

Chapter 1: Is paleo the best diet?

Our ancestors had a lot of things wrong, but not their diet. They had a balanced diet from the foods they hunted and gathered. From meats to quality veggies and fats, they made sure that nothing unhealthy entered their bodies. For this reason alone, the paleo diet is one of the most natural for the human body. As stated above, it is also the only diet that has stood the test of time and passed. If you apply all the guidelines of the diet with dedication, you are on the right track to achieving its benefits.

Many people are often interested to know whether or not the diet helps in boosting their general well-being. And those who opt to try it, do so for this sake. The answer is yes; it can help improve your health by a great extent. However, it doesn't move like a sky rocket. It is a process that takes time to deliver notable results. Therefore, you not only need dedication, but also patience and discipline.

The paleo diet is the best diet because it feeds you the basic nutrients you need, instead of junk. It also helps you to get rid of calorie-heavy foods that are mostly unhealthy. This will, in turn, need you to change most of your lifestyle and eating habits. You are most likely going to cut down your calories when you avoid junk and only feed on nutritious meals.

Chapter 2: Is paleo considered a low-carb diet?

Is it true that a paleo diet is low in carbohydrates? If that's the case, how does it vary from the ketogenic diet? Today, finding a gym or exercise facility that doesn't offer a paleo diet plan or ketogenic diets would be a miracle. The majority of people who are big fans of these two do so because they help them lose weight. A few others follow the diets for the health advantages. Whichever category you fall into, it is critical to have a thorough understanding of each diet before beginning. This will assist you in adhering to the latter's teachings.

The paleo diet focuses on consuming foods that cavemen ate in order to achieve maximum health. It makes the case that contemporary systems and foods are harmful to the human body. As a result, it is necessary to avoid consuming foods that are not from the early stages of development. This is supposed to enhance regular physiological functions, including digestion and other metabolic processes. Weight reduction and increased immunity are the effects of this improvement. Meat, nuts/seeds, eggs, fruits, fish, fats, oils, and vegetables are all expected to be consumed on a paleo diet. It's important to note that you can only consume certain oils and fats, not all of them. Olive oil, avocado oil, coconut oil, tallow, lard, and butter are some of the permissible variations.

Processed sugar, legumes, and wheat are among the items that have been excluded. So, at this point, it's easy to infer that the paleo diet is low-carb, which isn't far off the mark.

Although the low-carb aspect is not explicitly emphasized, this diet emphasizes protein and fats over particular carbs. As a result, it isn't necessary to be a rocket scientist to understand what this implies. Even a caveman understands that paleo does not eliminate all carbohydrates.

Grains and legumes are not allowed in the paleo diet since they were not available in the past. As a result, they contain antinutrients that are harmful to the body's health. Antinutrients are substances present in plant-based meals such as phytates and lectins, so if you're wondering what they are, here's an explanation. These chemicals prevent the body from absorbing nutrients and minerals. Furthermore, when consumed in excessive quantities, they might cause stomach problems. As a result, if you want to avoid them, you must do so.

Chapter 3: Benefits

Because the paleo diet is focused on complete, unprocessed foods, it's only natural to conclude that it offers several advantages. Anything that reduces artificial flavors, colors, additives, and preservatives helps to keep your health at its best. The paleo diet removes all of the aforementioned, as well as taste enhancers, sweets, sweeteners, and salt.

The paleo diet has a two-pronged effect. It reduces pollutants while also increasing the body's immunity and nutritional capacity. This is because it promotes the consumption of a variety of nutrients that may help make this a reality. The majority of those who have tried the program have reported increased muscle mass and weight reduction. Others praised the diet for its ability to improve metabolic processes and intestinal health.

The diet is high in fiber, which, when combined with water and a low salt level, helps to minimize bloating. The human gut flora is an important component of digestion, and when it is strengthened by food, digestion improves. Foods high in fat and protein increase satiety and minimize the amount of food consumed per serving. Have you ever noticed how quickly you get full after eating meat or fish?

The majority of today's ailments are referred to be "lifestyle diseases." They arise as a result of the way we live and consume on a daily basis. Cancer, diabetes, and obesity are examples of such illnesses. If you go far enough into the facts concerning cavemen, you'll discover that such illnesses never existed, even in their wildest hopes and fantasies. The sort of preservatives and mysterious chemicals utilized in today's meals are the root of the issue. No one would suffer from any of these ailments if they ate a totally healthy and natural diet. And paleo is the key to overcoming chronic disorders and leading a healthy lifestyle. The substantial rise in energy levels is likely to be the first advantage you will notice while on this diet. If you're dedicated enough, you'll lose weight as well. Here are some of the most significant health and well-being advantages of this diet:

It is quite normal.

Only the entire foods consumed by our forefathers – the cavemen – are used in a genuine and well-crafted paleo diet. And at this time, you should be aware that everything they ate was procured via hunting and collecting. At the period, the major sources of sustenance were wild fruits, edible greens, fish, and meat. This does not imply that you should put on a skin and go hunting for food in the woods, but it does imply that you should eat healthily.

Eating healthily entails consuming only meals that are high in nutrients. It also entails avoiding any processed meals and beverages that are devoid of nutrients. Instead, they will deplete the body's nutritious content. Meat, fish, and eggs, among many others, are examples of whole meals accessible today.

Environmentally friendly

It assures that nothing we consume has an environmental impact since it promotes natural eating. The majority of processed foods are harmful to the environment. So, if you're consuming nutrient-dense foods, keep in mind that you're also caring for the ecosystem.

Your body will have greater energy as a result of this.

Foods that feed the body make up the paleo diet. As a result, rather of consuming energy, they invest in it and increase its production. So, if you eat beef and spinach, for example, your body will have enough of energy to go through the day.

Reduces the amount of toxins in the body

This diet aims to eliminate toxins in the body by emphasizing natural foods over processed alternatives. Chemicals used in processed meals are responsible for the majority of the poisons. Food additives used in preservation are among them. Food was preserved by cavemen using several rudimentary methods that worked. We now have refrigerators that can help us store food thanks to technological advancements. As a result, you don't have to buy processed foods just because you want them to last a long time in the house. In fact, it is preferable to eat something fresh because it is less likely to cause harm.

Furthermore, the paleo diet encourages the consumption of antioxidant-rich greens. These antioxidants aid the body's removal of toxins and free radicals. Free radicals are a byproduct of metabolism, but they can be harmful in large quantities. They have the potential to cause cancer and other disorders.

Starting Paleo (Chapter 4)

Now that you've learned the basics of the paleo diet, it's time to figure out how to put it into practice in your life. Here's a guide to help you through the process:

Before you begin,

There are a few things you should know and do before diving into the paleo diet. Obviously, based on the preceding text, you are aware that the paleo diet is an antiquated variation from a previous era. Furthermore, in the past, people did not consume low-quality foods. As a result, before beginning the eating routine, you should remove all completely handled food sources. Following that, there are several things to think about:

Chapter 5: Guide

This is an important tool to have on hand if you decide to follow the paleo diet. It isn't always going to be a simple journey, despite what you may believe. You may be enticed to undermine your eating regimen at times, while at other times you may be enticed to completely abandon it. Similarly, people who are constantly on the move do not have a reliable location to prepare the paleo diet. Overall, how can one ensure that they are following their eating routine even when they are far away from home? This chapter deals with a wide range of issues.

Outside the house, Paleo

It's easy to get caught up in life, especially if you're working and constantly traveling. You may occasionally feel compelled to give the paleo diet a try, but you may not have the opportunity to do so. While it is correctly perceived as a reason, there are ways to help you pay attention to the call of paleo eating fewer calories in any case. When you're destroying from home, it often feels like you're in a minefield. You have no idea how the food was prepared, whether the menu was well-thought-out, or what the food looks like. These concerns may deter you from trying the paleo diet. It may even tempt you to eat unhealthy foods on a regular basis, which is far worse.

To see the benefits of any eating regimen, you should stick to it as much as possible. A paleo diet is no exception, and you should not hesitate to follow it while traveling or away from home. When trying to stick to a paleo diet outside of the house, it's always a good idea to call ahead or look at the menu before going. Make sure they have a plan in place for a paleo diet. This usually helps you avoid time pressure and stress from your friends or companions who may accompany you to the café. Because of the way they look at you while portraying the type of food you want, they may deter you from making your paleo request.

Another issue of eating paleo outside the house is the cost limitation. Sadly, many individuals accept that eating an eating routine a long way from home is too\sexorbitant to manage. While this is the famous thought, it isn't typically the situation. The paleo diet, to be more exact, is a reasonable choice to pick. There are various ways of making it much less expensive and more helpful in a hurry. Consider the accompanying tips that may enormously help you while on travel or away from home:

Use a healthy meal delivery plan. there are plenty of these out there, and you won't miss one that has your tastes. Don't always think that meal delivery is just for pizza, fries and other junk foods. Sometimes just change your order a little bit and focus on eating a healthy meal. The food delivery niche has, in recent years, exploded with new options and varieties of foods for their clients. Diets have also been an entrant in the food delivery business. Before ordering from any meal delivery company, make sure that you have carefully gone through their website and seen\s

their ingredients and nutritional info. Some may claim to offer paleo ready food, which might not be the case in reality. Also, while checking the ingredients, make sure that they are easy to recognize. A good tip eating paleo away from home is that you shouldn't buy what you don't know. At home, feel free to try out new paleo foods, but not while on transit. However, don't imagine that changing your order from junk to healthy paleo is sacrificing flavor for health.

There are numerous recipes and foods that follow the paleo guidelines and will still excite your taste buds.

Use available websites with sufficient information. While on the go, it is not easy getting a paleo friendly restaurant. It may be your first time in that area and so, you don't know a lot of places or people. Therefore, traversing the place in search of a healthy restaurant is daunting. Luckily, there are websites that could help make this easier for you. Some of them include Yelp, menupages.com and TripAdvisor. All of these sites can help you take a look at restaurants around your locality, that offer the paleo diet. You can then settle on one where you will go, or switch between different restaurants every day. This will make you have an easy time making your order because now you don't have to describe what you want to eat in detail. Simply check the menu, make a choice and wait for it to be brought.

It won't be perfect. Don't feel bad when you may miss a meal or two of the paleo plan while traveling. It is bound to happen and there isn't a lot of you can do to forestall that. It is assessed that an individual will possibly take around 80 percent of paleo when out of home. Consequently, when you pick an unfortunate nibble decision or miss a feast once, it won't kill you. The possibly reason to worry is the point at which this turns into a habit.

Always try to pre-eat. When you can, leave the house after eating a healthy paleo diet. This will help you stay away from other cravings while on transit. This is especially important if you are traveling for only a short while and you'll be back home. For instance, if you are traveling in the morning or afternoon and will be back in the evening, make sure that you have had enough food before departure. Also, if you constantly travel, you can make this a common practice before leaving.

Carry paleo snacks. Well, eating a dense breakfast alone isn't enough; you should equally prepare a few snacks for the road. Even when you're at work, you can feed on these snacks instead of eating unhealthy junk. Take time during your weekend rest and prepare sufficient snacks that will push you through the entire week.

Chapter Two

Pros and cons of paleo

Like In this wayme other thing on the planet, a paleo diet is more than a little flawed. It enjoys its benefits and deficiencies. It is basic to know both prior to beginning once again the eating regimen plan. Remember, this is a diet that is based on what our forefathers ate, over two million years ago. As this is the situation, it will undoubtedly have a touch of constraint. This is on the grounds that life in those days isn't equivalent to now. Notwithstanding, we can't likewise excuse the way that the stone age men carried on with a better life than we do. We can't affirm through research since it is restricted, however we can affirm for a reality that they did. They were less defenseless to infections and intricacies when contrasted with us. What's more the greater part of the illnesses we go through today, are because of the way of life we lead - this is reality. A few examinations have shown that our advancing way of life has prompted a few illnesses mankind faces today, like malignant growth and heftiness. So, what preferable method for safeguarding ourselves over doing what the cave dwellers did to survive?

The eating routine supports the utilization of entire food varieties in the spot of handled and unhealthy foods. This implies great wellbeing in any language. Notwithstanding, it likewise restricts the carbs you take in and this might cause a principal issue, mostly examined prior in the book. Along these lines, you want to find the turn and find some kind of harmony between the upsides and downsides of paleo that you will peruse here.

All of the food varieties that were absent in the paleolithic time are accepted to be perilous to the All in allundness of a person. The contention is that the body can't contain and separate handled food varieties. Thus, it is prudent to keep away from them in entirety. This may not be implausible as there is a trace of validity in it. Clinical investigations have shown that the body finds it difficult to process handled food sources and garbage. It is therefore that they attempt to support individuals from enjoying such eating regimens on a more regular basis. So, who is correct and who is off-base? Here is a glance at a portion of the known upsides and downsides of consuming a paleo menu or plan.

A larger part of the current populace needs supplements for ideal wellbeing. There are a few fundamental standards you really want to utilize while enhancing. Some of them incorporate the following:

Get your nutrients from food whenever you can – humans are naturally adapted to getting their nutrients from the foods they eat. Supplements are only a back-up, in case there is a low presence of nutrients in the body. The truth is that whole foods are better placed to give you the right set of nutrients than supplements will. For instance, lycopene is a supplement but doesn't meet the exact needs of the human prostate tissue like tomatoes do. So, only use supplements when you are unable to accrue the respective nutrients in foods.

Take natural nutrients whenever you can – synthetic nutrients don't have much effect in the body when compared to the natural variants. It does matter when it comes to the preparation of synthetic nutrients. Some are prepared through biological means while others through technological aspects. The downside of using industrially produced vitamins is that they don't have the same physiological actions as the naturally occurring types. For example, folate is not the same as folic acid, not in form and benefits. And as much as folic acid can be converted in the body to folate, the process is poor in man. As stated earlier, folate is important for the development of a healthy brain in the fetus. Folic acid, on the other hand, does not have the same benefits. In fact, it doesn't even cross the placenta, which makes it practically futile. The main outstanding advantages of folic corrosive in the body of a pregnant lady is that it forestalls neural cylinder deserts. Later examinations have shown that folic corrosive is a huge reason for malignant growth in the body and not folate. Normal folate is, be that as it may, costly and not generally utilized in multivitamins. But this doesn't mean that you cannot get it if you wish to.

Don't just take any supplement . So, it will get to a point where you might need to supplement your paleo diet. And multivitamins have constantly become very popular in recent years, especially in the western world. But you need to be careful as not all multivitamins are safe for the body. In fact, dieticians and experts argue that a huge majority of these multivitamins either have no benefits at all or even cause harm in the body. The problem with these substances is that they have so little of the basic nutrients needed in the body. And this can lead to a nutrient imbalance in the body, which ultimately causes diseases and other complications. Besides, most multivitamins use cheap and ineffective ingredients such as folic acid, which is not the same as folate. This not only fails to work in the body, but also causes a lot of other problems, as discussed.

So, regardless of whether you choose to involve the right enhancement for your supplement needs, for what reason would they say they are significant? Why is enhancing significant toward the day's end? Here are a portion of the reasons why:

To boost sleep quality. As discussed earlier on in the text, the paleo diet may cause some imbalances when it comes to sleeping patterns. And this normally arises due to the deficiency of some nutrients in the body. To correct it, you might have to use a dietary supplement for that particular nutrient that is deficient.

Because of the diversity of plants in the modern era. This is another reason why a supplement may make sense now more than ever before. In the past, there were rich soils and this facilitated the production of nutritious plants. Today, soils have been polluted with a lot of toxic substances, resulting in the production of less-nutritious plants. Supplements help to replace these lost nutrients. Furthermore, the cavemen usually ate their gathered fruits and greens raw. But on the contrary, we cook our greens, which even depletes them more of the basic nutrients.

Lack of sunlight exposure. How many kids go out to play nowadays? Even adults spend most

of their time inside houses. They rarely go out due to one thing that has enslaved all of us – technology. And going out means getting the sunlight, which is vital for the synthesis of vitamin D in the skin. Therefore, vitamin D supplements are recommended to solve this problem.

Due to the rise in environmental and lifestyle stress. This hampers the absorption of nutrients in the body, thus necessitating the use of supplements to recover.

The increased use of antibiotics and other drugs. Most of these drugs affect the presence of nutrients in the body by draining them. Supplements help to replenish the lost nutrients in the body.

A high exposure to toxins. Toxins are slowly becoming the order of the day in our modern world. The only hope now is to use supplements to guard the body against the depletion of nutrients.

Using a paleo diet is helpful to the body, and can work on your wellbeing however it isn't sufficient. You might in any case miss the mark concerning a few supplements, particularly the carbs. Consequently, you should utilize enhancements to recuperate from a lack of forthcoming. Here are a portion of the enhancements that you want to begin using:

Vitamin D

This is the fundamental enhancement required in the body, particularly in this day and age. People get this nutrient in two essential ways: from the food sources they eat and through daylight. The last option is a more significant wellspring of the two. Tragically, very few individuals get adequate stock of daylight. Also this may be the justification behind the lack of nutrient D.

You would expect that you can without much of a stretch remunerate daylight for food, however this won't work similarly. Regardless of whether you are utilizing a decent eating regimen like paleo, it is hard to acquire sufficient vitamin D without appropriate daylight. In this way, it is still extremely required to involve daylight as a hotspot for vitamin D. Overall, around 42 percent of the western total populace is lacking in this nutrient, which is close to a large portion of the all out populace. The nutrient is additionally imperative for most body processes and different advantages as well. A portion of the jobs it plays incorporate bone wellbeing, heart wellbeing and mind work. It is likewise a significant invulnerable booster.

The paleo diet depends on entire food varieties. A large portion of these food sources are quire nutritious thus, you will seldom have any requirement for supplements. However, this specific nutrient isn't bountiful in the paleo menu. Furthermore hence, you will require enhancements to add it to your present eating regimen. For the vast majority who run occupied plans consistently, gaining admittance to the sun is to a greater extent an extravagance as opposed to a need. The main time which appears to be feasible to gain admittance to this regular source is during get-aways. Furthermore this doesn't come consistently; it is intermittent.

Clearly, the cave dwellers didn't have this issue since they could invest the majority of their energy outside hunting creatures and assembling wild foods grown from the ground. Along these

lines, in fair treatment, they got steady admittance to the sun, uninterrupted.

For the human living in this day and age, you should enhance your vitamin D supplement utilizing nutrient D3 cases and cod liver oil. The way that the sun is continually accessible doesn't imply that it is to the point of providing all the vitamin D that your body needs. Once more, you should realize that there are a few impediments to how successful the sun functions. For instance, since vitamin D is created through the synthesis in the skin, problems such as obesity, inflammation and ageing can slow the process. Then again, there are a few actual obstructions to vitamin D blend through daylight because of expanded time spent inside and blockage from colossal structures. Accordingly, fundamental to take enhancements can help the levels of this nutrient. These enhancements will assist you with staying away from a defective stomach, battle dangerous developments, lessen osteoporosis, avert misery and reinforce bones.

It is basic first to get tried and advised of your nutrient levels prior to settling on supplements. Don't just choose supplementation without first stepping through an examination, you could as of now have adequate measures of that nutrient. Additionally, you should continually reevaluate these levels with your PCP. This is to empower an adjustment of dose in the event that it is required. Moreover, you really want to guarantee that the nutrient D3 supplement you are taking is protected - liberated from fake or unwanted fixings that will undoubtedly influence your health.

Chapter Three

Supplementation

Chapter 7:

It is vital to enhance the paleo diet, as a result of a lacks of few supplement. Supplementation is basic to managing the limits of the eating regimen. But dieticians may ask, is it really essential to supplement the paleo diet? After all, the cavemen didn't need them. In any case, there's that time factor, that things have radically changed from how they were a long period of time back.

There's been a significant change in the climate, to be more exact. Allow us first to investigate a portion of the fundamental changes that are available in the current world:

Pollution . Unlike in the past, there is massive pollution nowadays. Air pollution is particularly getting worse every day and is affecting how humans live.

Environmental hormone disruptors. These ones alter the body's functioning and behavior.

The change in soil and food . Pollution might have contributed to the depleted nutrients in the soil. And this consequently led to the low nutrient foods that we harvest these days. Therefore, this deficiency in nutrients has necessitated the use of supplements while on a paleo diet.

Technology . In the past, there was no technological aspect that affected the way people lived. Today, there are numerous new inventions that constantly affect the life of man. For instance, the many artificial lights and entertainment items affect how man sleeps. Conversely, due to the changes in technology, humans are constantly competing to stay indoors than outdoors. For this reason, they rarely do exercises or even walk as much as the cavemen did.

Therefore, due to the above rea

In this wayns and more, supplements are vital for optimal health, when using the paleo diet. However, you need to use your supplements wisely, or else stand to experience the risks emerging from poor usage. The vast majority get all they need from a supplement thick eating regimen. So, not every person would have to utilize an enhancement.

Likewise, you may be feeling the loss of certain supplements in the body, however this isn't sufficient motivation to utilize supplements. Here and there enhancements have a few restrictions. Here are some of them to note:

An overload is risky. Supplements need to be taken in optimal quantities, not so much and not so little. If you are unsure about the amount to take, then it would be wise to seek advice from the nearest medical doctor or dietician. One example of a harmful supplement, when used in high quantities, is calcium. It can result in cardiovascular diseases, among many other complications. Typically, calcium goes to the bones and teeth to fortify them. But an excess of it will go to the arteries and lead to plaques.

Your body might not absorb the supplement. It is not always the same for everybody when it comes to the use of supplements. Not that the failure to absorb it will harm you; it simply won't

help you. And this beats the logic behind why you took it in the first instance. There are some diseases which particularly make supplement absorption a tussle. For instance, inflammatory bowel disease makes it very hard to absorb iron in the body. So, you might take an iron supplement, but it won't help you as it will just come out of the body as it gets in.

You might need another nutrient as a cofactor. An example of this is that taking calcium supplements without the body having enough vitamin K2, may not help you with bone health and teeth development. This is due to the vital role vitamin K2 has in the body– directing calcium to the teeth and bones.

And most calcium supplements fail to contain this essential vitamin. A good thing to do would be to look for a supplement that has its cofactor present.

More doesn't usually imply better. Simply having more nutrients in the body, in the form of supplements, doesn't mean that they will be beneficial to the body. The body has a natural way of getting rid of what it can't use. And the excess supplements taken into the body may simply go out through urine. Thus, you should consult a dietician whether you really need supplements or not.

Sometimes the body needs the nutrient in its original state. For instance, folate is vital for brain health, especially for developing fetuses. However, taking a folate supplement doesn't guarantee the same benefits.

With this multitude of explanations above, you may be at go across streets. All in all, is it right to take an enhancement or not? Despite the fact that there are many motivations not to take a supplement, you could in any case require them at a certain point. Not all enhancements are terrible, simply some. All things considered, your body needs supplementation at times where the supplements are drained. But pundits would argue that the cavemen didn't take these supplements. All things considered, truth be told, they didn't, yet would you say you are a stone age man? All things considered, the many changes that have occurred and clarified above, require the utilization of enhancements for the body's ideal health.

The paleo diet isn 't straightforwardly an impersonation of what the mountain men did or ate. The way that we are continually presented to ecological disruptors, air contamination and garbage, is sufficient motivation to go to a few restorative lengths. What's more a portion of these remedial measures incorporate taking enhancements. On the off chance that these little tablets have a few advantages in the body, why not take them in.

Chapter Four

Magnesium

This is another nutrient that you cannot entirely get through dieting alone, even when on a paleo diet. It is significant for various substantial cycles, including energy creation, blood coagulating and muscle withdrawal. It is additionally useful for helping rest levels, making of new cells and other metabolic cycles in the body. Albeit not well-informed, it might likewise support the decrease of cerebral pains, gentle blockage, heart inconveniences and cramps.

Vitamin D3 and magnesium supplements work synergistically. Thus, it is prudent that you take the two of them simultaneously. But this doesn't mean that you will ignore magnesium rich foods; you will still need to use them. Probably the best magnesium food varieties incorporate swiss chard, spinach, pumpkin seeds, crude almonds and avocado.

This supplement is especially extraordinary for those going through consistent pressure in their psyches and bodies. In this way, routinely enhancing your eating regimen will assist you with expanding the degrees of magnesium, and gain the advantages from it. Albeit a test is critical to demonstrate in the event that you have a low presence of this supplement, you can likewise know this through basic cycles. For instance, assuming you notice that you have persistent migraines, feel feeble and exhausted, have a deficiency of hunger and experience an excessive amount of stoppage, you may be lacking in magnesium. In any case, you will in any case have to visit a specialist, on the grounds that these signs could suggest another infection or complexity. You can involve regular quiet as an enhancement for magnesium. It is drinkable yet can likewise be accessible in tablet mode.

According to dieticians and academics, there aren't many combinations in the body that compare to magnesium in terms of importance and overall health. This is because it is needed by more than 300 molecules, including proteins related to DNA, RNA, and ATP. It is also important in the cell layers and overall bone health because it aids in particle transport over the film surface. The main reason why magnesium is difficult to get from the foods we consume is because the list of food sources rich in it is also limited. It is mostly obtained through nuts and seeds, since these are the most notable sources. In any event, if you consume an excessive amount of these seeds and nuts, you risk ingesting an excessive amount of polyunsaturated fats. The second concern is the one discussed above, which demonstrates how soil changes have affected supplement accessibility. Basically, magnesium levels in food have been steadily declining due to a decrease in supplements present in today's soils. This clearly implies that if you are not increasing your magnesium intake in your diet, you are most certainly deficient in magnesium.

Magnesium deficiency in the body has serious consequences, some of which are better imagined than experienced. Furthermore, some of them have already been discussed in the previous section. It's not hard to find a cutting-edge virus in which magnesium has no role to play. Asthma, diabetes, hypothyroidism, hypertension, metabolic disease, and acid reflux are only a few of these diseases.

The majority of people choose chelated magnesium supplements. Malate and glycinate are used in several of these structures. These structures are significantly more absorbed than the others, and will thus have less accidental effects in the body.

Enzymes for digestion

These are significant when the body is unable to produce the required quantity of chemicals for food absorption. Absorption is a delicate interaction that must go smoothly in order for the supplements in meals to be properly absorbed.

When there aren't enough of the appropriate components in the body, food sits undigested in the stomach for a long time. For the absorption of certain nutrient kinds, specialized proteins are necessary. Amylase, for example, is predicted to break down carbohydrates in the same way as lipase breaks down fats and protease breaks down proteins. Because the paleo diet emphasizes proteins and fats, it's necessary to take supplements with a large foundation of their individual catalysts. However, you may also choose a single tablet that has all of these substances in a single package to get all of the benefits. You should review the ingredients list carefully to ensure that you don't consume any unpleasant substances.

Digestive catalysts are also important for persons who have more susceptible stomach-related systems than the average. The moment at which you detect a block-like impact within the abdomen is also a way to tell whether your stomach-related structure has a problem.

Vitamin K2 is a kind of vitamin that is found in

This is an important vitamin that is supposed to help calcium go to the right places, including the bones and teeth. Calcium gets into the supply pathways without it, causing a variety of problems, including calcification. The vitamin also aids in the prevention of heart infections and discomforts. This vitamin may be found in foods including liver, egg yolk, grass-fed beef, and natto.

This vitamin is perhaps the most important, despite being overshadowed. It performs a vast range of functions in the body, all of which would have been inexplicable if it hadn't appeared. Furthermore, it is not limited to calcium digestion. It also aids in the activation of proteins while also promoting cardiovascular health. Regrettably, the great majority are also deficient in this vitamin, necessitating supplementation to maintain levels. It's important to remember that vitamin K1 isn't the same as nutrient K2, despite the fact that they're often misunderstood. Green vegetables like collards and kale contain K1. A fraction of the K1 that enters the body is converted to K2, which is rather insignificant in humans. It might be crucial for the health of ruminants.

Vitamin A, also known as retinol, is another essential vitamin in the body that requires replenishment if levels are insufficient. It serves as a foundation for the body's many biochemical cycles. It is also necessary for mineral, protein, and water-soluble nutrient digestion. Another remarkable feature of this vitamin is that it is a powerful cell reinforcement that aids in the elimination of free radicals. These are compounds that are produced naturally as a result of digestion, but may be dangerous if they are available in high enough quantities. They may also cause certain illnesses, such as disease. As a result, vitamin A may be able to help prevent detrimental changes from occurring inside your body.

Vitamin An is also important for multiplication since it aids in the progression of a pregnancy from conception to birth. It also aids in the proper development of critical body parts like as the lips, eyes, nose, and teeth. More over a quarter of the population consumes less of this vitamin than the recommended amount. The vitamin is abundant in organ meats such as the liver. This might be one of the main reasons why so many people fail to assist it via their eating choices. Few people seem to like liver, and even if they do, they don't consume it on a regular basis, which is all the more reason why you'd need a supplement.

Vitamin A, according to certain dieticians and clinical professionals, may be harmful to the body. Is this, however, the case? The fact is that excessive doses of vitamin A are dangerous, but not at optimal levels. When there is an oversupply of it, it may cause a variety of issues, including osteoporosis. It's also worth noting that osteoporosis isn't the only indicator of a vitamin A deficiency. As a result, before taking any supplement for this vitamin, check with your primary care physician to see whether it is deficient. If you're lacking in this area, consider using cod liver oil as a supplement. The best thing about cod liver oil is that it also contains vitamin D, which protects against the adverse effects of vitamin A. As a result, you receive two benefits in one.

Fish oil is a kind of omega-3 fatty

This supplement has been around for a while and has received the approval of most health experts and dieticians. It features a slew of health benefits, including avoiding aggravation and preventing cardio-related entanglements. However, other academics argue that the benefits derived from real fish outweigh those derived from fish oil. However, it's still a fantastic supplement to take if you can't consume the real fish for any reason. Genuine fish offers a few health benefits that you should be aware of before abandoning it entirely in favor of pills. Generally speaking, some of the benefits of ingesting fish oil include the following:

Reduces the discomfort in the joints.

Increases the rate at which the body's metabolic activities occur. Reduces the chances of developing diabetes.

Enhances the body's capacity to burn fat. Insulin resistance is increased.

Reduces the likelihood of malignant tumors.

Reduces the risk of cardio-vascular disorders and consequences.

Vitamin C is a powerful antioxidant.

This is the most basic nutrient needed by the body in both ruminants and humans. If you're wondering why, it's because none of them can ordinarily manufacture the vitamin.

Furthermore, it is an important vitamin in the body since it aids in the formation and maintenance of glutathione. Glutathione is the most effective cell reinforcement in the body, assuming you've heard of it before but have no clue what it is. This nutrient is deficient in around 30% of the world's population. This percentage may further rise if researchers focus on those who follow a certain dietary plan, such as the paleo dinner plan. The elderly and people with chronic illnesses sometimes need higher doses of L-ascorbic acid than the general population.

It is difficult to get a significant amount of this vitamin alone from diet. Supporting the accessible levels may seem to be an improvement along these lines. Although not everyone can consume them, red peppers are an excellent source of this vitamin. If you can't consume red peppers, try supplements like garden of life raw C and 100 percent acerola powder instead. Both will help to increase the levels of L-ascorbic acid in the body, which will help to prevent scurvy and strengthen the immune system in general. The vitamin also aids in the production of collagen and the development of the body's connective tissues.

Melatonin

Melatonin is legitimately used in peppers, despite the fact that it is not a major enhancement needed in the body.

Still extremely important. It's best for those who have trouble sleeping or suffer from sleep deprivation. It is, nevertheless, critical for a variety of functions, including gastrointestinal health, metabolic health, and weight management.

Iodine

It aids in ensuring that the thyroid is functioning properly and at optimal levels. This supplement may be found in whole foods such as raw milk, eggs, and sea vegetables.

If you don't find them there, you may take potassium iodine pills as a supplement.

Chapter 8: Mistakes

The paleo diet in some cases has its difficulties that make it hard to follow. Being a mountain man diet, individuals will undoubtedly commit errors because of the sharp distinctions existing between antiquated times and contemporary times. Moreover, to blunder is human and no single being is great. The important thing is that you don't repeat the mistake, and rather learn from it going forward. The vast majority commit errors on the paleo diet during the underlying stages. Furthermore this is the sort of thing that happens to each and every other eating regimen.

Subsequently, don't surrender since you didn't hit the nail on the head the first time.

A typical method for knowing whether you are committing errors on any eating routine, and in addition to the paleo diet, is through observing your outcomes. If you notice that there are no changes in your health and body after a long duration, then it would probably mean that you are doing Thusmething wrongly. The not-so paleo propensities are not difficult to succumb to, particularly in the event that you have hardly any insight into the eating routine while beginning. For that reason it is suggested that you learn first prior to endeavoring anything. The same way you wouldn't fly a plane prior to learning the essentials is the same way with abstaining from excessive food intake. Additionally, everybody makes botches, even the most elite. So, these missteps are restricted to novices, yet in addition the specialists in the diet.

Sometimes you might commit paleo errors intentionally (which isn't right) or unwittingly (which is reasonable) (which is reasonable). Nevertheless, here are a portion of the normal mix-ups made by those rehearsing the paleo diet:

Eating too much meat

Going paleo isn't a rea

In this wayn to eat a lot of meats. Indeed, the mountain men would benefit from enormous lumps, yet they are stone age men and you are a millennial. In those times, they would benefit from a ton of meat, yet at the same time eat assembled products of the soil. Additionally, they were continually progressing and this assisted with consuming the fats put away in their bodies. Remember, we are not as active now, as they were then. So, it's absolutely impossible that we can eat a ton of meat and remain solid like they did.

Most individuals generally succumb to the falsehood that paleo limits carbs and emphasizes more on protein and fats. However much this might have a touch of truth in it, there's where individuals are educated to benefit from a boatload concerning tissue. Fundamentally, when you eat a lot of creature proteins, you put yourself at the gamble of getting a few ailments and confusions. Weight gain and corpulence are a portion of the dangers you stand to confront when you eat abundance meat items. The normal discernment is that the eating regimen just involves meat and fats, barring veggies and carbs. Sadly, this is just yet a solution for disappointment in the eating regimen. Your body can't flourish without adequate supplements gotten from greens and carbs.

The breaking point is eating meat once in a day, which is awesome for somebody on this eating\s

routine. Anything over this will hurt your wellbeing and ruin the potential advantages that can be accumulated from the eating routine. However, the most important aspect of it all is to limit saturated fats. Furthermore a decent method for accomplishing this is through consuming natural poultry and fish. You can eat these routinely, perhaps following a day or somewhere in the vicinity. But for red meat, try and limit it to around once or twice in a week. Additionally, you should ensure that it is lean, particularly grass-took care of for additional advantages. You can put yourself at the risk of getting serious ailments such as heart complications when you take excess meat.

The paleo diet is more with regards to quality protein rather than high protein. It won't help you assuming you have unnecessary proteins that have no advantages in the body. Maybe take little partitions and gain every one of the supplements and advantages that you need.

There is a misconception that paleo implies many meats. Try not to succumb to this snare and wind up destroying your wellbeing. A lot of anything great is terrible. Loads of meat, particularly red meat, continually ruin your wellbeing and achieve various circumstances like gout. The way that proteins are fillers and lift satiety doesn't imply that they are the best answer for abstaining from eating. Indeed, they are similarly extraordinary for digestion, yet just 33 percent of your plate ought to have this macronutrient. Restriction is key for meat. The best other option assuming you truly need to eat more protein is utilizing plant based sources.

Failing to eat sufficient fats

Fats are the fuel that run the body's energy needs, particularly when carbs are low. Normally, the body involves carbs for energy needs, yet when there is nearly nothing, as on account of the paleo diet, an option is utilized. In the underlying stages, the body will involve fats prior to going to ketones as a fuel source. Some\sindividuals stay away from fats and focus on protein and a couple of veggies. This won't work for you fittingly since the body needs fuel for energy.

Eating the wrong veggies

Not all greens are suitable for the paleo diet. Of the numerous paleo veggies, broccoli stands apart as truly outstanding to eat. However much the utilization of veggies is profoundly supported in the paleo diet, it additionally matters the sorts that you eat. There are a few veggies that you shouldn't eat by any means, when in this eating regimen. For the most part, you really want to keep away from vegetables and the accompanying greens fall under this gathering; edamame, green beans, snow peas and string beans. The eating routine expresses that these greens are related with negative wellbeing impacts in the body. Thusly, they ought to be kept away from since the cave dwellers didn't benefit from them. There are various paleo amicable veggies to look over thus, this is a misstep that is not difficult to correct.

Falling for paleo processed foods

Some producers will bundle food sources and guarantee that they are paleo cordial. Since the market is packed and there is no unmistakable method for telling in the event that a specific food\s

is protected or not, it would be fitting to disregard the bundled food sources totally. Try not to fall a survivor of marks on food sources guaranteeing that they are paleo well disposed, without gluten or weight reduction cordial. A large portion of these names are simple promoting methods to draw clients into buying the said items. You could even wind up disrupting wellbeing. A portion of these compounds that are very hazardous for human consumption. yourself rather than working on your food varieties have hurtful synthetic Even those that case to make paleo amicable tidbits probably won't have good intentions for you. A paleo cake is as yet a cake and could have the impacts of an ordinary sweet treat. In addition, a large portion of these paleo cordial tidbits cause your body to have an expanded water maintenance ability, because of the presence of high carbs accumulated from dried organic product. This isn't incredible assuming you're focusing on weight reduction. The greater part of them are additionally out of the set norm or scope of macros required in the eating routine. Also this can make an unevenness in your paleo dinner plan. Quite possibly the main thing to note while on a paleo diet is balance. As expressed before, it should be around 40/30/30. What's more this is additionally tied on how regularly you have your helpings.

You shouldn 't eat treats routinely, whether or not they are paleo amicable or not. Obviously, you can have cheats here and there, yet not\sconstantly. All things considered, even the stone age man had infrequent treats when he coincidentally found colonies of bees and took the nectar. Also this didn't influence his wellbeing that much, you know why? Since it was sometimes and not regularly.

Refrain from the sugary treats or else stand to deceive yourself that you are closely following the paleo diet. That may be a fat falsehood that you really want to recuperate from. These'paleo treats' are nothing unique in relation to the ordinary sweet treats that we enjoy each day.

Failing to eat enough greens

The paleo diet could accentuate more on fats and proteins, however this doesn't imply that veggies are good and gone. Regardless, they are significantly more significant because of their dietary advantages. By and large, a great many people eat too little with regards to greens.

Furthermore this could likewise be the justification for why there are not such countless veggie lovers on the planet. Obviously, you could contend that meat is more flavorful than kales. But look at what you are gaining from both. The kales have a greater number of supplements for your body than meat.

Often individuals accept that just including a piece of kale their plates will have an effect. This is too little to even consider having any effect on a rat, not to discuss a completely developed human. You want to take an adequate number of greens or none by any means, for your body to acquire the advantages. Furthermore a decent method for eating veggies is to somewhat cook them or eat them crude. Along these lines, you can acquire each of the supplements it has, without voiding some.

Strive to add veggies in each feast that you take, from breakfast to lunch and supper. If you can't add it to every meal, then consider eating them, at least, twice in a day. The same way paleo is tied in with removing grains, vegetables and dairy items is the same way it is tied in with having more veggies to supplant their space. Relinquish the possibility that vegetables should be a side dish. They are a vital part of the fundamental supper and ought to be treated as so. It is assessed\s

that veggies have multiple times the normal degrees of dietary fiber when contrasted with other food sources. In a word, eat a great deal of veggies.

Eating too many nuts and seeds

This is another barrier that the paleo adherents experience in their excursion. Indeed, nuts and seeds are significant in the body, however there's a cutoff. They might be delicious and even nutritious, but eating too many of them can cause problems, especially in your digestive system.

People have a very sensitive\sstomach related framework and hence, need to eat food varieties in constraint. A few food varieties eaten in huge bits can bring about blockage and stomach torments, among a few different intricacies. The human stomach can indeed deal with a limited number nuts, however not unreasonably. It can particularly deal with the non-crude, doused and grew nuts best.

Some nuts and seeds go about as enemies of supplements, as in they forestall the retention of certain supplements into the circulation system. The majority of the nuts and seeds that repress proteins from ingestion of supplements have two synthetic mixtures that make this a chance: lectin and phytic corrosive. These mixtures are normally more earnestly and more captivating for the body to process. Furthermore for that reason they additionally go about as inhibitors.

Failing to make up for the lost nutrients

The low admission of carbs and different food sources in the paleo diet is set to bring about supplement inadequacies. Also if you don't watch out, this can influence your body in numerous ways. The most dire outcome imaginable is the point at which you neglect to supplant the lessening supplements. Saying bye to vegetables, grains and dairy is certainly not a stroll in the park. It is certainly going to cause a lopsidedness and hole in your supplement proportions. As you will pass up crucial supplements, you should look for approaches to supplanting them.

In many cases, the most impacted supplements that are lost during a paleo diet incorporate; nutrients C, D and K2, dietary fiber and calcium. For dietary fiber, it would be fitting for you to take gigantic heaps of vegetables. Concerning different supplements, you can select dietary enhancements, if at all you can't eat the food sources that give them. A typical indication of supplement lack can be weight reduction, which might be deluding to anybody. You could believe that your body is beginning to get the full advantages of the eating regimen, yet this isn't true. You are just aggravating it through healthful starvation.

Before going full-time on the paleo diet, ensure that all your wholesome necessities are covered entirely. Over the long haul, you should consume more vegetables and new organic products to make up for the lost supplements. This will likewise assist with keeping up with your insusceptibility's solidarity so you don't miss out on sicknesses or contaminations. The verdant vegetables can likewise assist you a ton, particularly the dull ones with liking collard, kales and spinach. A portion of the non-dairy wellsprings of calcium that can likewise help you an extraordinary arrangement are cruciferous vegetables. A few instances of such veggies incorporate; broccoli, cauliflower and Brussels\ssprouts. With respect to vitamin D, rather than utilizing supplements, take additional time in the sun and furthermore eat rich food sources like egg yolks and mushrooms. This large number of\s

measures will assist with making up for any inadequacies and decrease your gamble of falling ill.

Chapter Five

Going to the extremes

Everything should be done in impediment. If not, you will gamble with influencing your wellbeing and obliterating your body's state. Alternately, the paleo diet should be done inside the given guidelines, no exaggerating nor underdoing. Tragically, the vast majority will generally go past these norms and onto limits. All things considered, going outrageous will just aggravate it for you, rather than the apparent enhancements in health.

Most individuals overdo it, where they totally dispose of specific nutritional categories from the eating regimen. One of the most regularly dispensed with nutritional category is the starch macronutrient. Since the eating regimen expresses that you shouldn't eat vegetables and grains, isn't sufficient motivation to leave carbs. They are still very essential in the body and help in energy creation, among numerous different capacities. There are various wellsprings of carbs, beside the confined grains and vegetables. Indeed, you can get carbs from different spots, including leafy foods. Along these lines, you really want to exploit the accessible sources, so you can reestablish the two essential sources that are prohibited. Completely disregarding carbs will bring about critical outcomes in the body.

Ignoring help and support

No man is an island - this is a typical maxim that is applicable to this specific case. Try not to accept that you can endure the paleo diet without the assistance and backing of experts.

Particularly when you are an amateur in consuming less calories, this is the time you really want assistance the most. You will undoubtedly commit errors and botches, with some that you're not mindful of. Having a dear companion, relative or even dietician to help you is really smart, particularly in the underlying stages. When you become acclimated to the eating routine and what it directs, you can happen by yourself.

Also, you should attempt to open up to individuals or your primary care physician, when you choose to try the eating regimen out. They are better put to exhort you on whether or not it is smart. Since it worked for your neighbor or companion doesn't imply that it will likewise work for your situation. Individuals have different dietary requirements and yours strength not permit you to utilize any eating regimen. Moreover, letting someone know could open up entryways for you to figure out how to utilize the eating routine and keep away from any missteps that would void it of the multitude of advantages. Likewise, figure out how to share any issues you experience while utilizing this eating regimen. Try not to keep calm when you begin to encounter abnormal signs and manifestations. You could excuse them as simple signs or indications, yet they can wind up to life compromise. Try not to experience alone when there are a few group prepared to help you whenever you really want assistance.

Another manner by which individuals disregard help from others is through the remarks made. Try not to put a hard of hearing ear to the worries of loved ones. At the point when they begin to gripe about something, view the objection in a serious way. They are the ones seeing your body and observing your wellbeing better. For instance, they might let you know that you are starting to lose a lot of weight, or perhaps you have begun having pale eyes. This can either be something

positive or negative, contingent upon the occurrence. Consequently, assuming you get such comments, it definitely should visit the closest clinic for additional advice.

Moral help is similarly vital, to guarantee that you don't abandon the eating routine. Once in a while it is the main thing you are let with when be. It can give you the impetus to move forward, even when you feel like giving up. Particularly while you're going through a full way of life change, it would appear to be legit assuming that you utilized the help coming from loved ones to convey on.

Support doesn't need to come from individuals you know, from family or companions. You can get support online through various consuming less calories discussions. For instance, there are various Facebook pages and gatherings that can truly be of incredible assistance when you are either starting or going through an eating routine. Instagram and Twitter additionally have networks that you can join and meet large number of individuals going through various eating regimens. You are rarely alone, particularly on account of innovation. The help you will get once you open up will be overwhelming.

Assuming that it is a weight loss plan

The paleo dinner diet isn 't a weight reduction plan, as many might suspect. Indeed, it can assist you with getting in shape, however that isn't its selling point. It is simply a healthy lifestyle trying to emulate what our ancestors did back then. It is just the standards of this diet that incorporate keeping away from garbage and handled food varieties, that might bring about you shedding pounds. Also this is basically out of your change in way of life, and not on the grounds that paleo is some enchanted pill that individuals use.

It is this suspicion that can make one abandon the eating regimen. You will continually have it at the rear of your psyche that you should get thinner inside half a month. Also in the event that this neglects to occur, you will begin to envision that it is on the grounds that paleo is a trick. Try not to be misled by special recordings that listen for a minute you need to hear. They will seldom express the method involved with abstaining from excessive food intake for what it's worth, since they realize it is thorough and requires some investment. What's more individuals really try to avoid processes that require some investment. But one thing for sure while using paleo, or any other diet for that matter, is that you must be patient. It is a progression of preliminary and disappointment until you begin getting the benefits.

Even assuming you are utilizing paleo exclusively to get in shape, which you can at any rate, don't expect the outcomes short-term. You will have to be disciplined and follow the diet even for an entire year or several months, to witness the benefits.

Ignoring fiber

Fiber is a fundamental piece of the human eating routine, despite the fact that it can't be processed. It is one of only a handful of exceptional substances that get into our bodies and isn't processed yet is as yet supportive. Individuals who consume fiber will generally have better lives than the people who don't. This simply shows how significant it is in the body. A high-fiber diet has as of late been connected with the generally safe of enduring heart sicknesses. Additionally, roughages likewise help in assimilation, and forestall clogging, among numerous different

confusions or illnesses. It is likewise significant as far as making preparations for metabolic syndrome.

So, how does fiber work in the body, since it isn't processed? Indeed, it takes care of the valuable microorganisms in the stomach, subsequently reassuring their increment in populace. It is these microorganisms that play an assortment of jobs in the body, including forestalling various sicknesses and conditions. You should take note of that an eating regimen that has colossal lumps of meat and has fats is altogether falling short on fiber. Also this is essentially what many individuals consume while on the paleo diet. Therefore, you need to look for extra sources of fiber from plants, which you will then incorporate in your diet.

Failing to plan

This must be the greatest obstacle that paleo devotees face, particularly prior to beginning the eating routine. Assuming you neglect to design nearly anything, you're making the ideal formula for disappointment. Staying with the eating routine isn't so much as an issue, so long as you have made a decent arrangement. It isn't exactly imaginable to awaken one day and guarantee you are prepared to begin the paleo diet; truth be told, it would be over the top, most definitely. Whenever you begin consuming less calories and don't have the foggiest idea what you should eat for each feast, you will become wasteful at following it. What's more for that reason the vast majority surrender to desires and different enticements. But when you have a well-crafted menu that dictates what you plan to eat for every meal, you are more likely to stay put on the diet for longer without getting tempted to satisfy your cravings.

Also, you want not disregard the way that you will require snacks on the way. Indeed, it is undermining the paleo diet. But isn't it better to cheat with paleo friendly foodstuffs at least? You will equally need to consider how everything will be when you're out of home. You may be following a mountain man's eating regimen, however this doesn't imply that you won't escape your home. Ooh pause, even mountain men emerge from their modest habitation to search for food. You ought to have an arrangement on how you will eat when out of the house, particularly assuming that you are a regular voyager or go to work on a more regular basis. Fortunately, we have examined this before on in the book, about paleo moving. Ideally, those tips will help you out not to wreck while eating out.

Going crazy on the baked snacks

They may be paleo agreeable, In any case this doesn 't eclipse the way that they are snacks and can really hurt your body, particularly when taken past cutoff points. There are various choices that case to be paleo well disposed. Also you may be enticed to utilize them consistently, which will wreck you. All that you do and eat should be with some restraint. It isn't terrible to have these treats, not under any condition, indeed, it is prudent to do as such. However, when you take an excessive number of them into your framework, you start to annihilate the establishment you battled such a huge amount to assemble utilizing the paleo diet.

Ignoring the quality of ingredients

Any eating routine should be followed stringently, incorporating the fixings utilized in anticipation of food. It is obligatory for you to check the names cautiously to ensure that you are utilizing the right fixings. Any deviation from the right fixings can bring about the entire eating regimen not helping you out. Bacon, for example, is one illustration of a food that has changed quality, contingent upon which type you purchase and where precisely you purchase. Pork and hamburger are likewise different instances of meats that can wreck you, contingent upon where you get them. A decent practice is to make it a propensity for purchasing meat just at dependable stores. Furthermore this likewise applies to different fixings that you will use in the readiness of your dinners. Stay away from any fakes as they can cause destroying effects.

Getting too hung up about the caveman idea

This is one thing that paleo bloggers and specialists in the eating less junk food field go wrong - overemphasizing on the cave dweller perspective. Actually there are sure things that our precursors did, which we can't do at the present time regardless of whether we wished to. They ate no handled food sources, didn't eat certain carbs, went hunting and assembling regular feeds. They did all that and more in light of the fact that, around then, there was no other option. The life in those days can't be likened to that which we live at this moment we can't even compare.

So, guaranteeing or accepting that you should follow the paleo diet precisely the manner in which the stone age man did is lost. You can follow a ton of what they did, yet not everything in entirety. Our progenitors didn't get the opportunity to experience synthetic compounds and additives in food sources, yet we do. They didn't find the opportunity to encounter less rich soils bringing about healthfully insufficient plants, yet you do. The varieties are immense to such an extent that you can scarcely expect twenty to thirty year olds to copy the paleo diet. Nonetheless, here you are told - don't go overboard.

Failing to sleep and exercise

The stone age men didn't simply lounge around sitting and hanging tight for the medical advantages of their eating routine. They continually got busy with various exercises, which guaranteed that they were dynamic all the time. Being dynamic assisted them with practicing and stay in shape. Also later on, they would have a rest and rest to recharge their bodies. Rest and practicing are imperative components of a paleo diet - and paleo, yet some other eating regimen. It would be trivial utilizing the paleo diet and neglecting to get adequate rest and exercise.

Obviously, dozing is for the most part achieved by numerous consistently, yet, you want to get sufficient rest. Not simply getting to bed for three hours or so and getting off. On the off chance that conceivable, go up to the standard eight hours that will ensure amazing rest. Then again, practicing is likewise very fundamental. Attempt and timetable a couple of hours in your day to one or the other run, run, walk or participate in exercise center related exercises. It assists with shedding off pointless fats in the body and water weight.

Not leveraging on technology

The way that the eating regimen in setting is from old times doesn't imply that you can't utilize

innovation to make it considered, the fundamental guideline around work better. All things paleo is development. Furthermore the way that development occurred implies that few things changed. It is, in this manner, unavoidable that innovation is something that has arisen and changedafter some time. Furthermore utilizing it to the upside of the eating routine is extraordinary. You can glean some useful knowledge, for instance, when you utilize various sites to explore the paleo diet. Even this book you are reading is a product of technology. Without it, you wouldn't have a hold of such a lot of data without any problem. Notwithstanding, don't allow innovation to take the better piece of your brain, to the degree that you neglect what's truly significant. Keep in mind, however much there is significant data on the web, a similar applies to trash filled information. All you really want to do is to find some kind of harmony between the two, and realize what is gainful to you.

When you don't have a good cause to eat paleo,

From beginning to conclusion, the reasons for your decision to follow the paleo diet will be explained. There isn't enough of a plan to get you through the diet. In all honesty, you must provide an explanation in your proposal. You can't just start eating paleo without understanding why.

A change in your eating habits will have an impact on your whole lifestyle. It's anything but a minor adjustment in this regard. To motivate you to keep going, you need a true goal. If you don't, you may as well give up. You'll almost certainly be forced to make a few decisions you've never considered before. When everything is said and done, old habits die hard - changing from your previous habits will take some effort.

The fear of becoming Along These Lines isn't enough incentive to start an eating plan and keep to it without giving up - there's simply not enough meat on the stick to convince anybody. Many people would have thrown out a lot of items, including drugs and rubbish, if they thought their health was a problem. As a result, we must accept that although health is important, it is not sufficient to push a person. To be honest, even looking better after following a paleo diet would not be enough to convince someone to try it.

As a result, before jumping into the paleo craze, do some soul searching. This can help you figure out why you need to slim down in the first place. You will almost always be given a reasonable explanation.

Detoxing with the paleo diet

A paleo diet isn't a way to get rid of toxins. It can indeed help you with this, but that isn't why you use it. Some people feel that by just changing their eating habits, they may become poison-free. Keep in mind that the body may absorb a variety of chemicals that are harmful and can lead to an increase in the level of toxins. The fact that you are eating whole foods rather than junk is enough encouragement to live a healthy lifestyle free of toxins. However, this does not guarantee that the ones within the body will vanish.

consuming an excessive amount of dried fruit

The sugar obtained from dried organic goods is processed by the human body in an unusual manner, especially when ingested without the water content of a typical natural food. Furthermore, you can eat more dried organic goods than you can while they're full of water. People prefer dried organic items since they are more convenient to consume. Consuming six mangoes in one sitting, for instance, is difficult. When the mangoes are dried, however, the process takes just five minutes.

Having a cluttered pantry

When you say your last goodbyes to your partner in a relationship, you must disconnect all links and correspondences. This will let the two players proceed more smoothly and easily. When either the accomplice is near by or both of you are still in contact, a test is normally anticipated to continue. You will be lured to stay where you are if you continue to see someone or something that you should move away from.

Similarly, if you truly have the old supply in your storage area, quitting your previous eating routines is tough. Some argue that as long as the food sources aren't used, everything is alright. The problem is that no one knows how long or strong your endurance is. Good for you if you can withstand seeing your favorite snacks and meals and yet refuse to consume them. However, if you are unable to tolerate, you should avoid certain meals and indulgences.

If you don't clean out your pantry, you're likely to consume non-paleo foods from time to time. It's also possible that you don't know you've made a mistake until after the fact. You could unintentionally ingest some bad cooking oil or another fix. Consider acquiring a special shelf or storage compartment if you can't get rid of non-paleo food variety in your pantry, maybe because you share it with someone else. In other words, you can't tolerate mixing paleo and non-paleo foods. Also, keep in mind how agonizing it might be to keep looking at things you can't eat.

Inadequate hydration

To be more specific, water is critical for calorie reduction. When you're in a routine, it may help you direct a lot of things that might go wrong. While water is the most important drink to consume, it is not the one to concentrate on. Other paleo-friendly beverages that quench your thirst while improving your health are also available. Make sure your refreshment menu doesn't include any beverages that have been artificially upgraded and managed. These often include a high caloric content and may completely destroy your structure. Green tea, black espresso, and, of course, plenty of water are among the permitted drinks. Creating a set of regulations that are much too rigid to be followed.

While abstaining from excessive food consumption, don't be too hard on yourself. At the end of the day, it's just a diet to help you live a healthier life. It isn't a sentence to indefinite suffering imposed by a prison judge. Again, take a look at yourself and determine your specific nutritional needs. If you believe you won't be able to stick to the diet, you're probably correct. Never, ever, ever, ever, ever, ever, ever, ever, ever, ever, ever, If you need to give up any of your favorite foods, be sure you're prepared to cope with any negative consequences.

Ignoring any allergies that may occur

The paleo diet isn't an optimal eating plan in the sense that it doesn't work for everyone. As a result, if you're unsure about your eating regimen, you should see a clinical professional or dietician. When you can't take it anymore, don't yield to paleo and let it dominate you. Specific sensitivities may restrict the kind of foods you may consume in some cases. Even if you're on a paleo diet, you should be aware of this allergic response. Because they are recommended in the diet, don't purposefully consume food kinds that stimulate your receptor levels.

Failure to consume sufficient amounts of good fats

In this eating plan, not all fats are beneficial to you. The wet versions are clearly dangerous and may lead to a variety of problems. What is a sound fat, anyway? What other ways do you think you'd be able to set yourself apart? Solid fats are those that have a low level of cholesterol or none by any stretch of the imagination, which should always be at the top of the priority list. They aid in the breakdown of various fats in the body, providing you with the energy you need throughout the day.

Overeating

As soon as possible, distinguish between calorie counting and fasting. Fasting and eating less carbohydrates have nothing in common. Furthermore, a lot of people make this mistake when they first start a diet. They recognize that the two terms are interchangeable. You can alter your diet, but you don't have to make drastic changes to get the benefits. Furthermore, fasting entails eating very little - far less than the bare minimum.

If you're on a paleo diet, eat to your extremity whenever you're hungry - but not excessively. You're good to go as long as you're consuming paleo-friendly cuisine and sticking to your daily goals. Consuming enough filler meals such as vegetables and dietary fiber is the greatest strategy to prevent feeling always hungry.

Beginner food plan (Chapter 9)

If you've ever wondered what paleo is or what it entails, now is the time to do so. As you may expect, this is not an arduous feast plan. It'll make your mouth swim and make you want to devour everything in sight. For your paleo start-up, here's a 7-day meal plan to follow:

the first day

BREAKFAST - Sausage Omelet Ingredients 3 large eggs Coconut oil is a kind of vegetable oil that comes

2 grilled turkey hotdogs green luxuriant greens of any kind

You'll be licking your fingers after eating this supper. LUNCH - Ingredients: mixed salad greens Sea bass, fried Seeds from a pumpkin Dressing: olive oil leaves for a salad

If you like vegetables, this is the perfect meal for you.

STEAK WITH ROSEMARY

The meat steak was taken care of with 200 grams of grass. 1 lemon-juice glass

2 garlic slivers

12 pepper 1 teaspoon sea salt 1 teaspoon sea salt 1 teaspoon sea salt 1 teaspoon sea salt 1 teaspoon sea salt 1 teaspoon sea

Prior to cooking with the other ingredients, marinate the hamburger steak in rosemary first.

The total number of calories you consume in one day is 1122, and the macronutrient breakdown is 124 grams of protein, 63 grams of fat, and 45 grams of carbohydrates.

The second day

INGREDIENTS FOR BREAKFAST – EGG CACAO

12 eggs are required

2 onions, 450g turkey sausage (ground)

12 peppers, green

The most popular number is mushrooms.

Reduce the number of mushrooms to five or less. This way, you can eat your dinner while still keeping your calorie intake under control.

LUNCH – Tuna salad with avocado and tomato Ingredients

12 avocados, medium-sized fish (80g), and spinach leaves (tinned)

2 to 2

This is a cross between a meat eater and a veggie lover. It tastes incredible and is perfect for satisfying your lunch cravings.

SALMON SAUSAGE WITH ASSORTS FOR DINNER

the seeds of sesame

lemon juice (glass) Olive oil that is 100% pure. Red peppers with mustard flavor Medium and gluten-free spinach salad sheep hotdogs Asparagus

This is the perfect dinner mix. Your dinner is ready to serve in just a few moments.

The total number of calories you consume in one day is 1310, and the macronutrient breakdown is as follows: 186 grams of protein, 77 grams of fat, and 56 grams of carbohydrates.

3.

ALMONDS AND BERRIES BREAKFAST Ingredients

5 pistachios

4 berries of blue 1 milk glass

This is a fantastic way to start your day with milk, berries, and almonds.

Ingredients for LUNCH – Super salad (Paleo)

two hard-boiled eggs

bubbled Balsamic vinegar

12 strawberries, sliced\s5 walnuts

A modest bunch of spinach leaves

Another incredible paleo super plate of mixed greens to require your as the day progressed and fulfill your hunger.

DINNER – Sweet potato with chicken Ingredients\s200g of chicken, barbecued 2 cups of spinach

1 cup of yam, heated 1 carrot

4 pecans Fresh basil

Sweet potato is exceptionally nutritious, particularly when blended in with delightful chicken. The all out calories you eat in this day will be 1410 while coming up next is the breakdown for the macros; 210g protein, 93g fat and 75g carbs.

Day 4\sBREAKFAST – Turkey bacon with pepper-baked eggs Ingredients\sCoconut oil 2 eggs

2 rings of pepper

2 cuts of turkey bacon

Doesn't the smell of bacon toward the beginning of the day just rouse you? LUNCH– White fish wraps

Ingredients Lime Coriander

½ an avocado, sliced 1 fish filet, barbecued A small bunch of lettuce

White meat is consistently a sound treat to water your taste buds during lunch hours.

DINNER – Mixed salad with tuna Ingredients\sA small bunch of blended salad 2 bubbled\s

eggs Olive oil\sTuna, canned

What a tasty method for finishing your day utilizing a superb feast of blended salad and tuna. The complete calories you eat in this day will be 1114 while coming up next is the breakdown for the macros; 97g protein, 43g fat and 25g carbs.

Day 5\sBREAKFAST – Berry smoothie Ingredients

glass of coconut milk 1 cup of blended berries A modest bunch of spinach

Who doesn't adore smoothies. The berry smoothie is an incredible approach to launch your day.

LUNCH – Tuna and salmon sashimi Ingredients

Some bean stew some basil 250g tuna

Some seaweed\scups of avocado salad

This flavorful Japanese treat will rule your taste buds for lunch. DINNER – Mexican chili and lettuce

Ingredients

½ some water A touch of pepper

1 teaspoon of ocean salt

1 tablespoon of tomato paste Some coriander seeds and cumin 1 teaspoon of paprika

3 cloves

1 onion, diced\s500g of meat, minced some carrots, ground some guacamole

Some lettuce and tomato salsa

This Mexican dish shuts the day with a bang of heavenly taste and fulfillment.

The all out calories you eat in this day will be 1967 while coming up next is the breakdown for the macros; 760g protein, 126g fat and 95g carbs.

Day 6

BREAKFAST – Turkey sausage scramble Ingredients

60g turkey hotdog, hacked 3 eggs, large

90g of Brussels sprouts 1 sweet potato

An awesome blend of delectability and wellbeing to get going your day. LUNCH– Seafood platter\sIngredients

4 oysters Some calamari

Some green plate of mixed greens 5 prawns, grilled

Why not have a sample of the ocean for lunch? The fish platter is an incredible pick.

DINNER – Lamb chops and spinach Ingredients

500g of sheep cleaves A cup of spinach

A cup of red cabbage, spiced\s½ red pepper Olive oil

Who doesn't cherish sheep slashes? A delightful method for shutting the day.

The absolute calories you eat in this day will be 1756 while coming up next is the breakdown for the macros; 520g protein, 123g fat and 99g carbs.

Day 7

BREAKFAST – Mushroom omelet Ingredients\sspring onions\stomatoes\smushrooms\s2 eggs

This omelet makes certain to set off your taste buds into beginning the day with joy.

LUNCH– Mixed salad with chicken Ingredients

1 avocado Olive oil A cup of blended salad 250g of chicken

A combination of salad and chicken is consistently a solid approach to dine. DINNER – Sunday roast\sIngredients

250g chicken, simmered 1 lemon Mustard

A cup of rosemary

A cup of carrots, cooked A cup of cloves

Mint Butter A cup of green peas and broccoli

This is an innovative method for shutting the week with a Sunday roast.

The all out calories you eat in this day will be 1546 while coming up next is the breakdown for the macros; 260g protein, 78g fat and 65g carbs.

The above dinner plan is not difficult to follow and the suppers won 't invest in some opportunity to get ready. Be mindful so as to pick the right fixings so you don't wind up wrecking your diet.

CPSIA information can be obtained
at www.ICGtesting.com
Printed in the USA
LVHW050559140422
716000LV00007B/382

9 781915 435002